~ *A* SEASON OF SUNDAYS *2001* ~

Images of the 2001 Gaelic games year by the *Sportsfile* team

of photographers, with captions by Tom Humphries

An Official GAA publication, published by Sportsfile

Photographers

Ray McManus, David Maher, Brendan Moran, Matt Browne, Damien Eagers,
Ray Lohan, Aoife Rice, Pat Murphy and Brian Lawless

Captions

Tom Humphries, The Irish Times

Photographers' Portraits

Joe Maher at GR Watts, Dublin

Design

The Design Gang, Tralee

Colour Reproduction

Colour Repro

Printed in Ireland

Future Print Limited

Published by

SPORTSFILE

Patterson House, 14 South Circular Road,
Portobello, Dublin 8, Ireland

ISBN: 0-9523551-5-9

ANOTHER INSIGHT INTO THE

GAMES OF THE YEAR

As we ponder the passing of another *'Season of Sundays'*, it is once again a great honour to be associated with this wonderful work from Ray McManus and the rest of the Sportsfile team.

Few publications are awaited each year with such anticipation, and it is a testament to the professionalism and endeavour of the Sportsfile photographers that this outstanding book is now entering its fifth edition and fast becoming a 'must have' for all Gaelic football and hurling fans.

It has been an intriguing year on the GAA fields. The new and innovative Football Championship was just a part of the overall story. From the raw passion of Club battles to the hope inducing performances of the League, through the spine-tingling excitement of the Provincial and All-Ireland Championships to the high fielding, high-octane ardour of the International Rules Series in Australia, there have been few constants. And yet week in and week out there was one thing we could depend on: the presence of Ray and his elite team.

Gaelic Games capture the very essence of what is best in Irish society. They are a huge part of what makes us unique. They embody the passion of a nation, our sense of local pride and our unquenchable appetite for honest sporting endeavour.

This book manages to portray all of these attributes, moments frozen in time but forever filled with wonder. It captures the joy of winning, the heartbreak of losing and that distinctive fulfilment offered by competing. It shows us the tension of the masses, the innocence of youth and the mutual respect among warriors of the game. More than anything else, this collection captures the defining moments of a season of progress for the Association and of superb entertainment for the fans.

This decorative and informative series will immortalise the season of 2001 for future generations. A picture, they say, is worth a thousand words. As you peruse this book you will find its many wonderful shots have captured - in a manner that words would struggle to equal - the excitement, passion, intensity and humanity that define our games.

To Ray and his team we say: Congratulations on another excellent production and the remarkable manner in which you have captured so many magical moments.

Go raibh míle maith agaibh go léir agus rath Dé ar an obair

Seán Mac Thaidhg

SEÁN MAC THAIDHG

UACHTARÁN, CUMANN LÚTHCLEAS GAEL

sportsfile

GREAT DAYS AND UNFORGETTABLE MOMENTS

BRENDAN MORAN

AOIFE RICE

BRIAN LAWLESS

DAMIEN EAGERS

MATT BROWNE

DAVID MAHER

PAT MURPHY

RAY LOHAN

RAY MCMANUS

It has been a year of abiding images, a year filled with moments, many of them tragic, which are burned forever into our memories. Strange isn't it that in a time when we have more media than ever before, more channels, more web sites, more of everything whether we want it or not, that it is the old fashioned photograph which endures best. In 2001 the worst of times and the best of times were recorded in so many different ways yet it is the stolen moment of a simple photograph which gives us most pause. A picture of grime faced firemen carrying their deceased chaplain from the rubble in Manhattan can move a person more than the endlessly looping footage of the moments which preceded this. It is an almost threadbare cliche but every picture tells a story.

These pictures are uniformly from the sunny side of the street. They are the moments of our diversion and pleasure through a hard year. Difficult times make us value these moments more I think. The images captured in here sing to us of the best that life can offer.

I am proud on behalf of the Sportsfile team then to present this collection of photographs from the Gaelic Games year of 2001. It was a notable year in so many positive ways, the football season grew to record size and hurling came back in all it's glory after a quiet season or two.

I hope that this collection of photographs will provide a fitting record of some great days and unforgettable moments. It is a collection for the good times, an album of pictures which will bring back memories of sunny days and simple pleasures.

What could be more valuable right now?

Carlow 0-05 Wicklow 2-15   O'Byrne Cup

NEW YEAR RESOLUTION. THE TERRACES ARE EMPTY, THE SKIES ARE PALE AND THE AIR IS COOL, BUT REFEREE SYLVESTER DOYLE STRIDES UNDETERRED ONTO THE PITCH FOR THE CARLOW VERSUS WICKLOW O'BYRNE CUP MATCH AT DR CULLEN PARK.

THE MAN WHO LIVES ON THE TURN JUST OFF THE INFORMATION SUPER-HIGHWAY. AS DUBLIN AND WICKLOW STRUGGLE TO THE END OF THEIR O'BYRNE CUP GAME AT AUGHRIM, THE SCOREBOARD OPERATOR TAKES A SEAT IN THE SUN. DUBLIN LOSE.

Wexford 1-11 Dublin 1-07 Walsh Cup

AND THE GUYS IN THE BLUE JERSEYS, THAT'S US. DAVEY BILLINGS SHOWS THE ROPES TO THE NEW DUBLIN HURLING MANAGER, KEVIN FENNELLY, AT THE WALSH CUP MATCH AGAINST WEXFORD AT FERNS.

Eircell GAA All-Stars Exhibition Game   **2000 All-Stars 9-14 1999 All-Stars 5-16**

STILL LIFE: RAINBOW FROM SUNCROFT IN THE DESERT WITH WATER. SWEAT ON HIS BROW, SAND ON HIS COLLAR, ANTHONY RAINBOW OF THE 2000 ALL-STARS GETS RELIEF FROM THE DESERT SUN AT HALF-TIME DURING THE GAA ALL-STARS EXHIBITION GAME AT THE DUBAI RUGBY GROUND.

ALL STARS AND GREAT SHEIKHS. JAMES HORAN GAINS POSSESSION FOR THE 1999 ALL-STARS DURING THE EIRCELL GAA ALL-STARS EXHIBITION AT THE DUBAI RUGBY FOOTBALL GROUND. THE ALL-STARS ARE PLAYING INTO THE DESERT END.

February 11

"Like your cap."
"Thanks! Nice coat you've got there."
"Tell me, where d'you get those lovely shoes?"
At Duggan Park, Ballinasloe, two umpires cut from the same cloth adjust the net prior to the start of the Galway v Clare game.

Galway 0-12 Clare 0-09   Allianz National Hurling League

An image that could define league competition — worth seeing but not worth going to see. Outside Duggan Park, Ballinasloe, a spectator clambers onto a bin to catch the closing stages of Galway's tussle with Clare.

March 3

AIB All-Ireland Club Hurling Semi-Final Replay   **Graigue Ballycallan 0-00 Sixmilebridge 0-00**

Victim of the coming plague. Foot and mouth disease swept these islands with biblical ferocity. Sport was among the first pleasures to be sacrificed. This afternoon, at precisely this moment, the ball is supposed to be thrown in here at Semple Stadium for the eagerly awaited All Ireland club semi-final replay between Graigue Ballycallan and Sixmilebridge. Instead only a shadow encroaches on the field.

Birr 3-21 Seir Kieran 1-9   Offaly Senior Hurling Final 2000

SIGN OF THE TIMES. HEADING OUT ONTO THE PITCH AT ST BRENDAN'S PARK, BIRR, FOR THE 2000 OFFALY COUNTY FINAL, THE BIRR PLAYERS NEGOTIATE A DISINFECTANT MAT.

April 15

*WHEN YOUTH HAS FLED AND POSSIBILITY HAS FADED, ALL WE CAN DO IS WATCH AND
ADMIRE AND REMEMBER. IN ARKLOW, AS THE LEINSTER HURLING CHAMPIONSHIPS GET OFF
TO AN EARLY START, THE KILDARE PLAYERS TAKE THE FIELD UNDER SEASONED GAZES.*

Wicklow 2-16 Kildare 5-11   Guinness Leinster Hurling Championship Qualifier

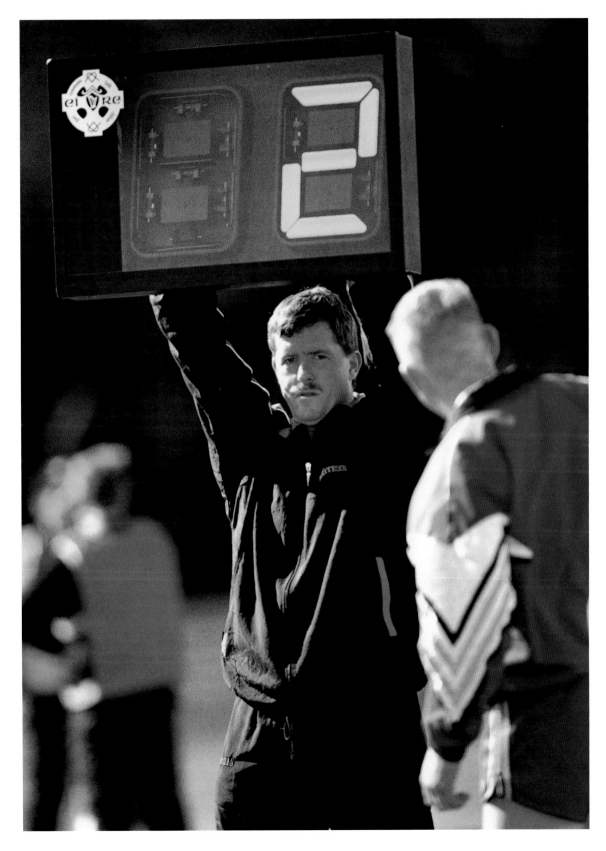

SIGN OF THE TIME. THE GAA CLOSES THE DOOR ON THE ERA OF CONTROVERSIAL DRAWS BY INTRODUCING DIGITAL CLOCKS TO TELL THE WORLD HOW MUCH INJURY TIME IS TO BE PLAYED AT THE END OF EACH HALF. HERE, IN AN EARLY EXPOSITION, THE FOURTH OFFICIAL, JOE KELLY, HOLDS THE FABULOUS DEVICE ALOFT AT THE END OF THE FIRST HALF. A WICKLOW SUBSTITUTE GAZES IN WONDER — OR PERHAPS THINKS THE CORNER-BACK IS BEING SUBSTITUTED.

Allianz National Football League **Galway 1-18 Kerry 2-09**

Athenry 3-24 Graigue Ballycallan 2-19 AIB All-Ireland Club Hurling Final

"I LIFTED THE FIRST HURL I SAW — IT WAS ONLY AFTERWARDS I REALISED IT WAS TOO LIGHT TO BE MINE." AND THAT WAS HOW THE WEST WON. IN THE LAST MINUTE OF NORMAL TIME IN THE ALL IRELAND CLUB FINAL, ATHENRY'S WONDERBOY EUGENE CLOONAN PERFORMS HIS LATEST MIRACLE, SCORING THE GOAL THAT IS A LIFELINE FOR HIS TEAM AND THE GRACE NOTE ON HIS CONTRIBUTION OF 1-11. HE SCORES DESPITE THE ATTENTIONS OF JAMES RYALL AND USING THE HURL OF BALLYCALLAN'S PADDY O'DWYER. THE GOAL BRINGS THE GAME INTO EXTRA TIME — AT THE END OF WHICH ATHENRY WIN.

ON A GREASY AND ANONYMOUS DAY IN TUAM, THE BOYS FOR THE LONG ROAD MAKE THEIR INTENTIONS CLEAR. JOE BERGIN, WHO WILL WIN AN ALL IRELAND MEDAL COME SEPTEMBER, RISES THAT LITTLE BIT HIGHER THAN WILLIE KIRBY, WHOSE SUMMER WILL END THAT LITTLE BIT SOONER.

April 16

THE CLUB IS THE CLUB IS THE CLUB. VICTORIES ARE SWEETER AND DEFEATS ARE HARDER. EDDIE O'DWYER OF GRAIGUE BALLYCALLAN IS CONSOLED

AFTER THE FINAL WHISTLE IN THE ALL IRELAND CLUB FINAL IN CROKE PARK.

Athenry 3-24 Graigue Ballycallan 2-19   AIB All-Ireland Club Hurling Final

IN ATHENRY, WHERE HURLING WAS REBORN TWO DECADES OR SO AGO, THEY HAVE MANY TEAM PICTURES THAT REPRESENT MILESTONES IN THE CLUB'S PROGRESS. FROM NATIONAL SCHOOL TO CROKE PARK, BOY TO MAN, JOE RABBITTE'S FEATURES BEAM OUT FROM SO MANY OF THEM. PART OF EVERY BREAKTHROUGH, THERE FOR GOOD DAYS AND BAD. JOE RABBITTE WAS ON THE FIRST ATHENRY TEAM TO WIN VIRTUALLY EVERYTHING FROM UNDER-ELEVEN UP. IT ENDS HERE, LIFTING THE TOMMY MOORE CUP ON BEHALF OF HIS HOME PLACE. HE HAS KNOWN NO BETTER DAY.

AIB All-Ireland Club Football Final   **Crossmolina 0-16   Nemo Rangers 1-12**

FOR SOME REASON THE CLUB CHAMPIONSHIPS RARELY FALL TO CITY TEAMS ANYMORE. NEMO, ONCE THE MONARCHS OF THIS GRADE, FOUND THAT OUT THE HARD WAY IN THE SPRING. PERHAPS IT'S THE PASSION BORN OUT OF COMMUNITY THEY LACK. MEN WHO COME FROM SMALL PLACES SEEM TO CARE MORE. JAMES NALLEN OF CROSSMOLINA IS FIRST AND HIGHEST; MAURICE MCCARTHY OF NEMO SHADOWS HIM.

CROSSMOLINA'S MOMENT. A GOOD YEAR FOR FOOTBALL WEST OF THE SHANNON BEGINS WITH TOM NALLEN LIFTING THE ALL IRELAND CLUB CHAMPIONSHIP TROPHY. BY THE END OF SEPTEMBER, THE NATIONAL LEAGUE AND ALL IRELAND TITLES WILL ALSO HAVE GONE WEST.

AIB All-Ireland Club Football Final   **Crossmolina 0-16   Nemo Rangers 1-12**

SEAN O'BRIEN OF NEMO RANGERS LOOKS BACK OVER THE LONG JOURNEY FROM CORK COUNTY CHAMPIONSHIP FIRST ROUND TO CROKE PARK. SOMETIMES THE MOST ARDUOUS JOURNEY IN FOOTBALL ENDS WITH NO REWARD.

PADRAIG BRENNAN OF KILDARE SAMPLES THE QUALITY OF HIS HOSIERY DURING HIS SIDE'S DIVISION TWO SEMI-FINAL GAME WITH CORK AT NENAGH.

April 29

Allianz National Football League Division Two Final   **Westmeath 3-11 Cork 2-13**

MATCH LOST, JERSEYS SWAPPED, TIME TO TALK ABOUT SUMMER. CORK PLAYERS AIDAN DORGAN (LEFT) AND EOIN SEXTON CONSIDER THE NEAR FUTURE IN THE AFTERMATH OF THEIR DIVISION TWO FINAL DEFEAT TO WESTMEATH.

FOR MANY PEOPLE, WESTMEATH WOULD BECOME THE STORY OF THE GAELIC FOOTBALL SUMMER AS THEIR FLOWING FOOTBALL AND DELIRIOUS FANS ANNOUNCED THEM AS GENUINE CONTENDERS. WITHOUT SO MUCH AS A PROVINCIAL TITLE IN THEIR CV, THEY LAID DOWN A MARKER FOR THE YEAR ON A GREY DAY IN APRIL, WHEN THEY HAD THE NOVEL EXPERIENCE OF WINNING A SENIOR COMPETITION IN CROKE PARK. THEY WOULD GRACE THE STADIUM SEVERAL MORE TIMES BEFORE SEASON'S END.

April 29

Old rivals shift their business to Croke Park. The National League title was destined to go west from semi-final time, when four Connacht teams remained standing. Galway and Mayo made it to the final. Here Seán Óg de Paor dives to take receipt of a ball ahead of Fergal Costello of Mayo.

ON A DAY OF NOVEL WINNERS, MAYO TAKE THEIR FIRST NATIONAL TITLE IN 31 YEARS. NOEL CONNELLY LIFTS THE CUP.

Allianz National Hurling League Final   **Tipperary 1-19 Clare 0-17**

Tipperary 1-19 Clare 0-17   Allianz National Hurling League Final

WITH A BACK SO STRAIGHT YOU COULD LAY YOUR GOOD CHINA ON IT, NIALL GILLIGAN STEADIES HIMSELF FOR A SIDELINE CUT.

NOT FOR THE LAST TIME. TOMMY DUNNE RAISES THE SILVERWARE AFTER TIPPERARY WIN THE NATIONAL LEAGUE FINAL.

May 13

A FLASHBULB POPS, THE MASCOTS APPLAUD, AND ALL IRELAND CHAMPIONS GET THEIR SUMMER SEASON UNDERWAY. SEAMUS MOYNIHAN, FOLLOWED BY MAURICE FITZGERALD, LEADS OUT KERRY.

Donegal 1-16 Fermanagh 2-13   Bank of Ireland Ulster Football Championship

STEPHEN MAGUIRE OF FERMANAGH GETS AHEAD OF EAMON DOHERTY OF DONEGAL IN THE FIRST OF THE SUMMER'S MEETINGS BETWEEN THE COUNTIES.

May 13

Bank of Ireland Leinster Football Championship Qualifier **Wicklow 2-06 Carlow 1-09**

WITH THE NUMBERS RUNNING AGAINST HIM, JOHN MCGRATH OF CARLOW FIGHTS A LOSING BATTLE FOR POSSESSION. DARREN COFFEY, GARY JAMESON AND BARRY SHEEHAN OF WICKLOW BACK EACH OTHER UP.

THE CHERRY BLOSSOMS ARE OUT, THE SUBWAY SIDINGS ARE BUSY, THE MANHATTAN JASPERS GRIDIRON TEAM ARE ON HOLIDAYS, AND THE TRICOLOUR FLIES BESIDE THE STARS AND STRIPES. IT CAN ONLY BE GAELIC PARK IN COUNTY NEW YORK. SCOREBOARD OPERATORS GET READY FOR THE MEETING OF DOWN AND NEW YORK.

CALLING ALL MASSEURS! CALLING ALL MASSEURS! JOB OPPORTUNITIES IN THE NEW WORLD! BRING US YOUR WARM OILS, YOUR HUDDLED MUSCLES YEARNING TO BE KNEADED! TEAMS OF HANDS SET TO WORK MASSAGING THE NEW YORK PLAYERS BEFORE THEIR CHAMPIONSHIP GAME AGAINST DOWN.

RUMBLE IN THE BRONX. GARY GORDAN OF DOWN PULLS ON THE BALL WHILE THE HURL OF NEW YORK'S BRIAN MCCABE MAKES CONTACT WITH HIS KNEE.

Bank of Ireland Ulster Football Championship   **Tyrone 1-14 Armagh 1-09**

Tyrone 1-14 Armagh 1-09 Bank of Ireland Ulster Football Championship

*IT AIN'T OVER TILL THE BIG MAN SINGS. FINBARR MCCONNELL, THE
TYRONE GOALIE, OFFERS UP HIS ARIA OF JOY ON THE CLONES TURF .*

*TRIUMPHALIST ORANGE MAN SEEN IN CLONES.
A YOUNG ARMAGH FAN BLOWS HIS TRUMPET WHILE
POSSIBILITIES STILL EXIST FOR HIS FADING TEAM.*

May 27

Bank of Ireland Leinster Football Championship **Dublin 2-19 Longford 1-13**

*"This Dublin team is ready to explode,"
roared Darren Homan after this
convincing win over Longford. Even if
it was thus primed, Kerry and Meath
had few problems in defusing. Homan,
however, arrived as a convincing
midfield presence. Here he gets a hand
to the ball ahead of David Hanniffy.*

*Incoming! Incoming! Peter Reilly of Cavan
levitates as he dispatches the ball from
the penalty spot during his sides
championship clash with Down at
Casement Park. Michael McVeigh starts
in the wrong direction but saves.*

May 27

SUMMER DOESN'T BEGIN UNTIL THE FIRST CHAMPIONSHIP SHOCK. HERE IT WAS. LIMERICK, REBORN WITH FEISTINESS AND VERVE, TAKING CORK IN THE PARK. CIARAN CAREY AND ALAN BROWNE STRETCH FOR ONE THAT GOT AWAY.

BACK IN THE SPRING, CIARAN CAREY DECIDED TO RETURN. HE LEFT BEHIND THE COLD WORLD OF RETIREMENT AND HIS HEADFUL OF DEMONS AND ONCE AGAIN LAID HIS SUBLIME SKILLS AT THE DISPOSAL OF HIS COUNTY. ALL SUMMER AS LIMERICK PROGRESSED CAREY GREW SWIFTLY TOWARD HIS FORMER STATURE. HERE HE IS EMBRACED BY HIS PATRICKSWELL COMRADE EOGHAN MURPHY AFTER LIMERICK'S DEFEAT OF CORK.

Bank of Ireland Leinster Football Championship   **Meath 2-12 Westmeath 1-14**

Galway 0-14 Roscommon 2-12   Bank of Ireland Connacht Football Championship

"WORRIED?" SAID SEAN BOYLAN "IT TOOK ALL OUR EXPERTISE AND GUILE TO GET US THROUGH BY THE SKIN OF OUR TEETH." THE SOLDIER AND HIS GENERAL. WITH THINGS SUPRISINGLY TIGHT ON THE FIELD OF PLAY, GRAHAM GERAGHTY OF MEATH TAKES A MOMENT TO CONSULT WITH SEAN BOYLAN. GERAGHTY'S INFLUENCE WILL BE CRITICAL. HE SCORES THE GOAL THAT KEEPS MEATH IN TOUCH AND MOVES TO MIDFIELD FOR THE FINAL TEN MINUTES.

COUP. ROSCOMMON GOALIE DEREK THOMPSON LEAPS INTO THE AIR, CELEBRATING HIS TEAM'S FAMOUS AMBUSH OF GALWAY AT TUAM STADIUM.

June 3

MILES TO GO, AND PROMISES TO KEEP, BEFORE THEY SLEEP. TIPPERARY HURLERS EAMON CORCORAN,
RIGHT, PAUL KELLY, CENTRE, AND CONOR GLEESON WALK OUT IN THE PRE-MATCH PARADE AT
PÁIRC UÍ CHAOIMH AT THE START OF THEIR HURLING SUMMER.

FOR MANY PEOPLE TOMMY DUNNE WILL GO ON TO BECOME THE HURLER OF THE YEAR. IN JUNE HE GAVE AN EARLY SAMPLE OF HIS FORM TO COLIN LYNCH OF CLARE, WHO IS DISPOSSESSED HERE.

Guinness Munster Hurling Championship **Tipperary 0-15 Clare 0-14**

Tipperary 0-15 Clare 0-14 Guinness Munster Hurling Championship

"THAT WAS SOME SERIOUS HURLING THERE."
NICKY ENGLISH KNOWS THE METABOLISM OF THE COUNTY THAT
NURTURED HIM, KNOWS WHEN THE PRESSURE IS ON AND WHEN
THE PRESSURE IS OFF. BEATING CLARE IN EARLY JUNE? A MAN IS
ENTITLED TO LEAVE THE SHADOW BEHIND AND DANCE ON THE AIR.

"WHATEVER UP WE GOT FROM JOHNNY COMING ON, WELL, WE LOST IT FAIRLY QUICKLY," SAID NICKY ENGLISH.
HARDLY ANYBODY IN TIPPERARY HURLING IS AS BELOVED AS JOHNNY LEAHY. WITH THE GAME HANGING ON A
THREAD IN PÁIRC UÍ CHAOIMH, NICKY ENGLISH PLAYS HIS TALISMAN. AS LEAHY JOINS THE FRAY, THE STADIUM
ERUPTS. THERE IS A SENSE OF DRAMA ABOUT EVERYTHING HE DOES. HIS ENTRY SAYS SOMETHING. GAME ON.
CLARE'S OWN RAIN-MAKER IS BRIAN LOHAN. THE THOUGHT OF THE TWO MEN CLASHING WITH THE GAME
GOING TO THE DEATH IS WHAT MAKES HURLING GREAT.
SIXTY SECONDS OF THUNDER. THEN JOHNNY LEAHY BURSTS FOR THIS BALL, ARRIVING BEHIND LOHAN. HE
FALLS AWKWARDLY AND RIPS HIS CRUCIATE LIGAMENT. SHOW OVER — BUT THE RESIDUE OF HIS INSPIRATIONAL
ARRIVAL WILL SUSTAIN HIS COMRADES.

June 9

Bank of Ireland Football Championship Qualifier   **Louth 0-13   Tipperary 1-08**

MOMENTS FROM GAA HISTORY. IT IS JUST BEFORE 3:30 ON SATURDAY JUNE 9TH 2001 AND TIPPERARY AND LOUTH GATHER ON THE SWARD AT CLONMEL, THE FIRST TIME TWO TEAMS FROM DIFFERENT PROVINCES HAVE MET SO EARLY IN THE SUMMER. ALL OTHER FIXTURES BEGAN AT LEAST HALF AN HOUR LATER. MEN BRAVELY GOING WHERE NO MEN HAVE GONE BEFORE? GERRY KINNEAVY IS THE REFEREE, LIAM CRONIN (TIPPERARY) AND NICKY MALONE (LOUTH) ARE THE CAPTAINS. SO NOW YOU KNOW. NO NEED TO PHONE A FRIEND. NO NEED TO ASK THE AUDIENCE.

SATURDAY NIGHT'S ALRIGHT FOR PLAYING. AGAINST THE BLUE OF AN EARLY EVENING SKY AT WEXFORD PARK, WESTMEATH'S RORY O'CONNELL FIELDS AHEAD OF TEAM-MATE BRIAN MORLEY AND WEXFORD'S WILLIE CARLEY.

SUMMERTIME AND THE LIVING IS EASY? AFTER 16 MINUTES, WATERFORD HAD AN 11-POINT LEAD. EVERY FORWARD OF THEIRS HAD SCORED FROM PLAY. PAUL FLYNN HAD RETURNED TO FORM, SCORING WATERFORD'S SECOND GOAL AS THEY STRETCHED THE LEAD AND THEIR LIMBS AGAINST LIMERICK AT PÁIRC UÍ CHAOIMH. NOT A CLOUD IN THE SKY AND NOT A WHISPER OF COMEBACK. WHAT COULD BE SWEETER?

Limerick 4-11 Waterford 2-14 Guinness Munster Hurling Championship

SUMMERTIME AND YOUR FEET DON'T TOUCH THE GROUND.
LIMERICK HAVE ROLLED BACK THE ROCK AND BRIAN BEGLEY
CELEBRATES HIS SECOND AND LIMERICK'S FOURTH GOAL.
A BURST OF THREE LIMERICK GOALS IN SIX MINUTES TOWARD
THE END HAS SWEPT WATERFORD AWAY.

June 10

EMPEROR OF THE AIR. WEXFORD SUBSTITUTE KEN FURLONG HOVERS ABOVE DECLAN CONROY OF LAOIS AND CONTEMPLATES HIS NEXT TRICK, PULLING ON A MOVING SLIOTAR.

HE WENT THATAWAY! REFEREE MICHAEL CURLEY AWARDS A FREE KICK WITH THE ABLE ASSISTANCE OF RORY GALLAGHER OF FERMANAGH.

Guinness Leinster Hurling Championship **Kilkenny 3-21 Offaly 0-18**

Dublin 1-12 Offally 0-13   Bank of Ireland Leinster Football Championship

June 17

WITH THE GAME JUST STARTED, MICHAEL BOND OF OFFALY AND BRIAN CODY OF KILKENNY WISH EACH OTHER WELL BUT ALLOW THEIR EYES TO CHASE THE SLIOTAR.

REDEMPTION SONG. NOT TOO LONG AGO THE INTER-COUNTY FOOTBALL CAREER OF DUBLIN'S PEADAR ANDREWS STUTTERED BADLY WHEN OLLIE MURPHY HOLLOWED HIM OUT IN A LEINSTER FINAL. PEOPLE WONDERED WHY THE DUBLIN MANAGEMENT PERSISTED. THIS YEAR THEY DISCOVERED WHY. ANDREWS HAD A GENERALLY IMPECCABLE SEASON. HERE, HE AGAIN BEATS OFFALY CAPTAIN COLM QUINN TO THE BALL.

June 17

Bank of Ireland Ulster Football Championship **Tyrone 3-07 Derry 0-14**

AT CLONES ALL MANNER OF NEIGHBOURLY FEUDS ARE DUSTED DOWN EVERY SUMMER. SOME OF THEM TWICE EVERY SUMMER. DERRY AND TYRONE HAVE NEVER BEEN LOST IN ADMIRATION OF EACH OTHER. HERE, STEPHEN O'NEILL CELEBRATES AFTER SCORING A KEY GOAL.

ARMAGH HAVE BEEN CIRCLING THE BIG TIME FOR A COUPLE OF SEASONS — BUT AN ALL IRELAND HASN'T FOLLOWED ON THE HEELS OF CROSSMAGLEN'S CLUB SUCCESS. AFTER A WINTER OF DISCONTENT, THEY STUMBLED INTO THE QUALIFYING JUNGLE DURING THE SUMMER. STEVEN MCDONNELL CELEBRATES AFTER SCORING ONE OF THE GOALS THAT PUT AN END TO THEIR JITTERS AGAINST MONAGHAN IN ROUND TWO

Monaghan 0-10 Armagh 2-12   Bank of Ireland Football Championship Qualifier

July 1

Guinness Munster Hurling Final   **Tipperary 2-16 Limerick 1-17**

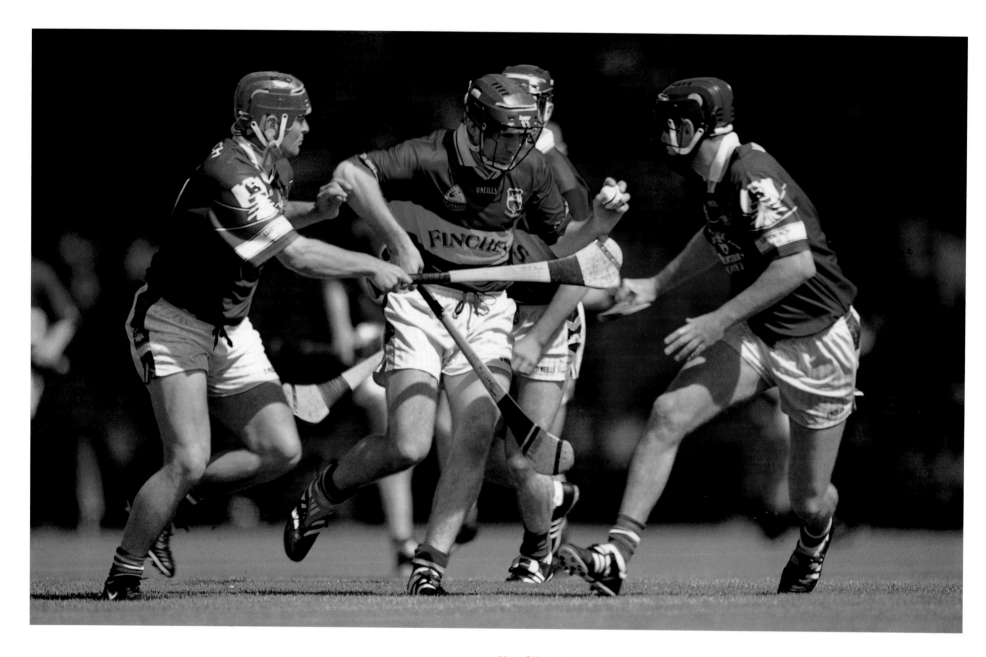

MARK O'LEARY'S SUMMER BEGAN SMALL AND BLOSSOMED MIGHTILY. ON MUNSTER FINAL DAY, HE SWIPED THREE POINTS FROM BENEATH THE STORM CLOUD THAT WAS MARK FOLEY. SO IT WENT — FILCHING SCORES HERE AND THERE, HEWING WOOD AND DRAWING WATER. ALL THE WAY TO A FAMOUS ALL IRELAND FINAL.

Tipperary 2-16 Limerick 1-17   Guinness Munster Hurling Final

*"Now we'll go up to play like a Tipp team
should play in Croke Park."*

*It's been eight years since a Tipperary man
lifted the Munster senior hurling trophy.
Forty years since a Toomevara man lifted
it. Tommy Dunne closes both circles after
his side's victory over Limerick.*

DAYS LIKE THESE ARE THE STAFF OF GAA LIFE. MAYO AND ROSCOMMON, SHOULDER TO SHOULDER,

NECK AND NECK, ALL THE WAY TO A FIREWORKS-LIT FINISH AT HYDE PARK. HERE, STEPHEN

CAROLAN OF MAYO IS A FINGERTIP AHEAD OF ROSCOMMON'S JOHN WHYTE.

Long time coming. Roscommon's first Connacht title in ten years tasted sweet. They have beaten Galway and they have beaten Mayo. Fergal O'Donnell, team captain, hoists the cup and is in turn hoisted on the shoulders of his countyfolk.

"BEST CONNACHT FINAL EVER? WELL, OF COURSE IT IS. I'D SAY ANYTHING AT THE MOMENT THOUGH."

AS PLAYER, COACH AND TEACHER, JOHN TOBIN HAS KNOWN MANY BIG FOOTBALL OCCASIONS IN CONNACHT. TODAY, THOUGH, THE GALWAYMAN HAS BROUGHT ROSCOMMON TO AN UNLIKELY HEIGHT. MINUTES EARLIER, OUT ON THE HYDE PARK PITCH, 21-YEAR-OLD GERRY LOHAN HAS RIFLED A 74TH-MINUTE GOAL INTO THE MAYO NET. TOBIN IS DRAINED, INCREDULOUS AND HAPPY ALL AT ONCE.

Laughing last and laughing longest. Michael Donnellan had a rollercoaster summer. He left the Galway panel at one stage. Came back as a first choice midfielder. His evident contentment was pivotal to Galway's improvement as the season matured. Here he celebrates Galway's squeaker of a win over Armagh.

THINGS CHANGED LAST SUMMER. NOWHERE MORE SO THAN IN SLIGO. NOTING THAT NOBODY EVER WON ANYTHING WHILE WEARING WHITE, THE COUNTY CHANGED COLOURS. UNDER THE MANAGEMENT OF MAYOMAN PETER FORDE THEY GOT TO CROKE PARK FOR THE FIRST TIME IN 26 YEARS. THEY WON TOO. BEAT KILDARE. AFTERWARD THEY WERE TOLD TO REVERT TO THEIR ORIGINAL — WHITE — JERSEYS. TOO LATE! A COUNTY HAD FALLEN IN LOVE WITH ITS NEW LOOK. YES, THEY WON BY A POINT. KILDARE WORE THEIR TRADITIONAL WHITE.

Sligo 0-16 Kildare 0-15 Bank of Ireland Football Championship Qualifier

SIGHTS FROM A SUMMER OF DEFIANCE. EAMON O'HARA'S CLENCHED-FIST CELEBRATION IN CROKE PARK. EAMON O'HARA BURSTING THROUGH THE MIDDLE TIME AFTER TIME. EAMON O'HARA FULL STOP. SLIGO, A MAN DOWN AFTER NINE MINUTES, HAVE JUST BEATEN MICK O'DWYER'S KILDARE. SOME PERSPECTIVE: LAST TIME THEY WERE IN CROKE PARK IT WAS 1975 AND THEY LOST BY 17 POINTS TO MICK O'DWYER'S KERRY.

Bank of Ireland Ulster Football Final **Tyrone 1-13 Cavan 1-11**

Tyrone 1-13 Cavan 1-11   Bank of Ireland Ulster Football Final

*BIG MAN FOR THE BIG OCCASION.
THE ULSTER FINAL ENDS. TYRONE
ARE TRIUMPHANT, BUT THEIR
GOALKEEPER, FINBARR
MCCONNELL, FINDS A QUIET
MOMENT IN WHICH TO CONSOLE
PETER REILLY OF CAVAN.*

*NAPOLEON AT CLONES.
DESPITE SUFFERING AN ARM INJURY
THAT FORCED HIS WITHDRAWAL,
TYRONE CAPTAIN SEAN TEAGUE
IS NOT GOING TO BE DENIED HIS
MOMENT IN THE SUN.
SINGLEHANDEDLY HE LIFTS THE
ANGLO-CELT CUP.*

Guinness Leinster Hurling Final   **Kilkenny 2-19 Wexford 0-12**

ON A DAY WHEN KILKENNY CASUALLY UNDERLINED THEIR SUPERIORITY YET AGAIN, ONE OF THE FEW HINTS OF WHAT WEXFORD STILL HAD IN THEIR HEARTS WAS THE PERFORMANCE OF DARRAGH RYAN AT FULL-BACK. TALL, ROBUST AND GAME, HE WAS A FULL-BACK BY TEMPERAMENT BUT NOT BY TRADE. INSERTED INTO THE POSITION AFTER A RASH OF INJURIES, HE MADE IT HIS OWN AND EMERGED AS ONE OF THE PLAYERS OF THE SUMMER. HERE, HE USES HIS STRENGTH TO EVICT DJ CAREY FROM THE DANGER AREA.

Kilkenny 2-19 Wexford 0-12   Guinness Leinster Hurling Final

THE COMFORTS OF ROUTINE. KILKENNY WIN THEIR FOURTH
LEINSTER HURLING TITLE IN SUCCESSION. DENIS BYRNE DOES HIS
DUTY AND LIFTS THE BOB O'KEEFFE CUP. NO SMILES. NO SONGS.
JUST TACKING A COURSE TOWARD BETTER PLACES.

Cork 1-13 Kerry 0-19   Bank of Ireland Munster Football Final

KERRY ARE SELDOM PERTURBED BY EARLY SETBACKS. SIXTY-SEVEN MUNSTER TITLES IS THE STATISTIC THAT EXPLAINS WHY. FULL-BACK SEAMUS MOYNIHAN GOES WHERE MANY KERRYMEN HAVE BOLDLY GONE BEFORE — INTO THE RECORD BOOKS AS A MUNSTER-TITLE-WINNING CAPTAIN.

HOPE ERUPTS. THE TERRACE AT PÁIRC UÍ CHAOIMH BECOMES A SEA OF RED AND WHITE, A CACOPHONY OF APPLAUSE, A GREAT, UNIFIED ROAR AS CORK TAKE A SURPRISE EARLY LEAD IN THE MUNSTER FOOTBALL FINAL.

Bank of Ireland Leinster Football Final   **Meath 2-11 Dublin 0-14**

Meath 2-11 Dublin 0-14   Bank of Ireland Leinster Football Final

MEATH'S SUMMER MAY HAVE BEEN A SEARCH FOR THEIR BEST FORM, BUT STILL THEY STAYED AHEAD OF THE POSSE NEAR HOME. TREVOR GILES LIFTS THE LEINSTER TROPHY.

AT TIMES IN THE LEINSTER FINAL, DUBLIN FELT SO CLOSE TO MEATH THAT THEY COULD TASTE THEIR SWEAT. AND YET MEATH'S SENSE OF CALM CONFIDENCE IN WHAT THEY WERE DOING WAS SELDOM SHAKEN. IN THE AFTERMATH, JOHNNY MAGEE OF DUBLIN TRIES TO FIGURE IT ALL OUT.

Guinness Ulster Hurling Final   **Derry 1-17 Down 3-10**

FAIR-HAIRED BOY. ODHRÁN MCKEEVER, THE SON OF DERRY STALWART KIERAN MCKEEVER, PLAYS HURLING IN THE SUNSHINE AT CASEMENT PARK PRIOR TO THE ULSTER FINAL BETWEEN DERRY AND DOWN.

THROUGH THE STRING OF LITTLE HURLING TOWNS SCATTERED ACROSS DERRY, THE GAME MAKES A COMMUNITY. COLIN MCELDOWNEY OF BALLINASCREEN CAPTAINED DERRY THIS YEAR. IN HIS MOMENT OF TRIUMPH, HE HAD A THOUGHT FOR HIS FRIEND AND SOMETIME RIVAL EMMET MCKEEVER OF KEVIN LYNCH'S IN DUNGIVEN. MCKEEVER WAS LAST YEAR'S CAPTAIN BUT, BECAUSE OF SUSPENSION, MISSED THE JOY OF LIFTING THE SILVERWARE. THIS YEAR BOTH MEN SHARED THE DUTY.

July 21

Bank of Ireland Football Championship Qualifier   **Mayo 0-16   Westmeath 1-14**

July 21

WESTMEATH IN THE DREAMTIME. IT'S A ONE-POINT GAME, A SMALL PIECE OF FOOTBALL
HISTORY FOR WESTMEATH — BUT FOR ONE FAN THE DAY HAS ALREADY BEEN TOO MUCH.
WEIGHTLESS BUT NOT SLEEPLESS, SHE SETTLES DOWN.

ONE SMALL STEP FOR MANKIND; ONE GIANT STEP FOR WESTMEATH MAN.
THE WONDER OF WESTMEATH'S SUMMER IS JUST BEGINNING TO UNFOLD BY THE TIME THEY MAKE THE
UNFAMILIAR JOURNEY TO DR HYDE PARK IN ROSCOMMON FOR THE FOURTH ROUND OF THE QUALIFIER SERIES.
FERGAL MURRAY FLOATS WEIGHTLESS ABOVE THE GROUND AS COLM MCMANAMAN LOOKS ON IN AWE.

Bank of Ireland Football Championship Qualifier   **Mayo 0-16 Westmeath 1-14**

SWEET RELEASE. LUKE DEMPSEY, THE WESTMEATH MANAGER, LETS THE TENSION ESCAPE AFTER THE FINAL WHISTLE AT DR HYDE PARK.

Derry 1-14 Cavan 2-07   Bank of Ireland Football Championship Qualifier

Eight years ago (can it be?) Anthony Tohill and Gary Coleman soldiered together to a famous All Ireland win. Much has happened since then: a team of great promise sundered; a parade of managers found wanting. This summer, though, had the feel of old times. Eamon Coleman's hands at the wheel; Gary Coleman playing well; Anthony Tohill back to his best. One day in Clones, the final whistle went on a fourth-round qualifier game and they realised they'd battled their way back to where they started. Another neighbourly tussle with Tyrone. That's what summers are for.

Bank of Ireland Football Championship Qualifier   **Dublin 3-17   Sligo 0-12**

THE WONDER OF CHAMPIONSHIP IS THE ENDINGS. FOR EVERY TEAM, EXCEPT ONE, A BAD DAY WILL COME. HERE, PAUL DURCAN LAMENTS SLIGO'S SUMMER, WHICH HAS JUST BEEN BURIED IN CROKE PARK'S HALLOWED TURF.

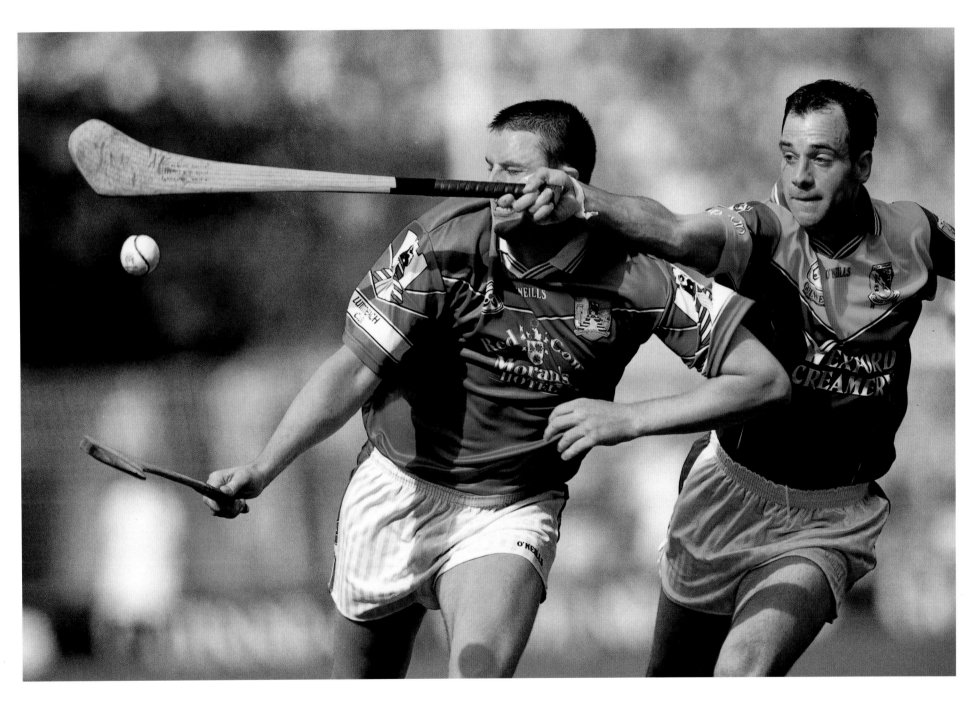

TWO TEAMS ON STEEP LEARNING CURVES MET IN CROKE PARK IN LATE JULY. A YOUNG LIMERICK SIDE, PICKING UP BATTLE SCARS ALONG THE WAY, AGAINST A REHABILITATING WEXFORD TEAM WHO HAD BEEN DISCOUNTED EARLIER IN THE SUMMER. BRIEFLY HERE, LIMERICK HAVE THE EDGE AS BRIAN BEGLEY SHIELDS POSSESSION FROM THE TENACIOUS DARRAGH RYAN.

Guinness All-Ireland Hurling Quarter-Final   **Wexford 4-10 Limerick 2-15**

Kerry 1-14 Dublin 2-11   Bank of Ireland All-Ireland Football Quarter-Final

August 4

'HE JUST COMES UP AND SWINGS FOR THEM,
LIKE THE BOLD FITZHENRY THAT HE IS,' SAID
LARRY O'GORMAN AFTERWARD. HERE,
WEXFORD GOALIE DAMIEN FITZHENRY
SCORES THE FIRST OF HIS TWO PENALTIES
AGAINST LIMERICK. MARK FOLEY IS AMONG
THOSE GUARDING THE LINE.

'YOU TALKIN' TO ME? I SAID, YOU TALKIN' TO ME?'
THE TRIP OF THE SUMMER AND ONE OF THE SIGHTS
OF THE SUMMER. DUBLIN MANAGER TOM CARR AND
REFEREE MICHAEL CURLEY HAVE A NOSE-TO-NOSE
EXCHANGE OF WORDS AFTER CURLEY AWARDS A
FREE TO KERRY LATE IN THE QUARTER-FINAL GAME
IN THURLES. THE INCIDENT INCITES A DUBLIN
COMEBACK AND INVITES A SIX-MONTH
SUSPENSION FOR TOM CARR.

A SEASON OF SUNDAYS *2001* **89**

WHAT GOES AROUND COMES AROUND AND WHAT'S GONE AROUND HAS JUST COME AROUND AGAIN. ROSCOMMON GOALKEEPER DEREK THOMPSON HAS HAD A GOOD SUMMER BUT TODAY GALWAY HAVE BITTEN BACK. HE GATHERS HIS GLOVES AND HAT, SLUMPS AGAINST THE POST IN MCHALE PARK, CASTLEBAR, AND BEGINS TO THINK ABOUT NEXT YEAR.

HE ARRIVES WITH SIRENS BLARING, THROWING HIS SHOULDERS AROUND LIKE THEY WERE SHOT PUTS. YET HE ALSO DOES THE JOB. VINNY MURPHY SCORES DUBLIN'S OPENING GOAL IN THE ALL-IRELAND QUARTER-FINAL AT THURLES.

Bank of Ireland All-Ireland Football Quarter-Final **Derry 1-09 Tyrone 0-07**

SIGN OF THE TIMES? FIFTEEN PLAYERS. FIFTEEN PHOTOGRAPHERS. DERRY LINE UP AND SAY 'CHEESE!' BEFORE THEIR QUARTER-FINAL WITH TYRONE AT CLONES.

RUNNING REPAIRS. KEVIN MCCLOY OF DERRY HELPS TEAM-MATE SEAN MARTIN LOCKHART

THROUGH A TOUCH OF CRAMP IN THE QUARTER-FINAL CLASH WITH TYRONE

Bank of Ireland All-Ireland Football Quarter-Final   **Meath 2-12 Westmeath 3-09**

SOME 73 MINUTES GONE, A THREE POINT LEAD, AND WESTMEATH PEOPLE HEAR THE WORDS THEY DREAD. GILES! TO GERAGHTY! TO MURPHY! GOAL! OLLIE MURPHY'S SECOND GOAL OF THE AFTERNOON LEVELS THE ALL IRELAND QUARTER-FINAL BETWEEN MEATH AND WESTMEATH AND ADDS ANOTHER CHAPTER TO THE GREAT CHRONICLE OF MEATH COMEBACKS.

Off the hook. Kerry goalkeeper Declan O'Keeffe celebrates with Mike Hassett after Kerry beat Dublin in their replayed quarter-final in Semple Stadium.

Declan Ryan is the golden thread. He made his debut back in 1988, back in the time when Tipperary still knew famine. He marked his arrival — and his determination to stay — with an All Star. Thirteen years later, he is the pivot around which two other newcomers revolve. Eoin Kelly and Lar Corbett have grown into the senior game as his protégés.

Oh, and Declan still provides a threat himself. Here, he gets his shot away even as David O'Connor, Wexford's promising corner-back, bends his hurl around Ryan's.

Radio Larry O crackles to life. 'Ah bro, how yez. Don't know where that came from but I'll tell ye, when ya play Tipp ya take yer breaks.' One of the heroes has a good day. Larry O'Gorman celebrates his second goal as Wexford set about bridging the gap that saw them eight points down with 25 minutes left.

Guinness All-Ireland Hurling Semi-Final Replay   **Tipperary 3-12 Wexford 0-10**

YOU MAY APPROACH THE BENCH.

Galway 2-15 Kilkenny 1-13   Guinness All-Ireland Hurling Semi-Final

FIND A PLACE TO PARK YOURSELF, FIND A SPOT OF
PEACE, GATHER YOUR THOUGHTS AND ADD ANOTHER
DAY TO THE DAYS. MR BILL KELLY FROM BALLYCUMBER,
COUNTY OFFALY, READS THE GAME PROGRAMME
BEFORE THE GALWAY V KILKENNY SEMI-FINAL AT CROKE
PARK. IN SEPTEMBER, MR KELLY WOULD ATTEND HIS
131ST ALL IRELAND FINAL, HAVING MISSED ONLY THE
POLO GROUNDS GAME IN 1947 SINCE HE BEGAN
ATTENDING FINALS IN 1936.

Guinness All-Ireland Hurling Semi-Final   **Galway 2-15 Kilkenny 1-13**

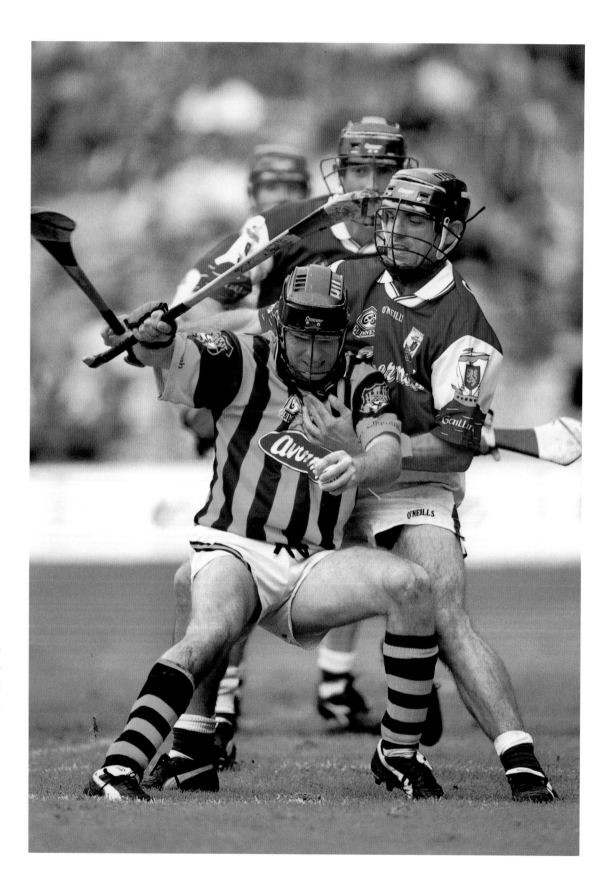

AND HOW WAS YOUR DAY, DJ? ON AN AFTERNOON WHEN THE KILKENNY FULL-FORWARD LINE WAS SUPPOSED TO PROVIDE AN EXHIBITION THAT WOULD COPPERFASTEN ITS CLAIMS TO GREATNESS, THEY FOUND EVERY ROAD CLOSED. EVEN DJ CAREY, PEERLESS FOR SO LONG, RAN INTO STOP SIGNS. HERE, MICHAEL HEALY OF GALWAY HAS BACK-UP IF NEEDED.

'Our second goal? It was a lucky ball that just came in high. I just got a boot to it.' For a lad who is so pathologically shy of publicity and so resolutely modest in conversation, Eugene Cloonan sure gets called upon to explain a fair number of miracles. Today, without being flash, he has scored 2-9 on Kilkenny.

IN REAL LIFE, NOEL LANE IS A QUIET, UNDEMONSTRATIVE MAN. REAL LIFE BEARS NO RELATION, HOWEVER, TO BEATING KILKENNY BY FIVE POINTS IN CROKE PARK ON A BIG DAY.

*JARLATH FALLON OF GALWAY, STRUGGLING TO
ESCAPE INJURY ALL SUMMER, DEFIES GRAVITY AND
PAIN TO CONTEST THIS HIGH BALL WITH JOHNNY
MCBRIDE OF DERRY. DECLAN MEEHAN LOOKS
ON AND WAITS FOR THE BREAK.*

Bank of Ireland All-Ireland Football Semi-Final   **Meath 2-14 Kerry 0-05**

A HUSH FALLS ON THE MEATH DRESSINGROOM. ALL HEADS TURN. PÁIDÍ Ó SÉ IS AMONG THEM. NEVER IN THE 18 YEARS OF SEAN BOYLAN'S REIGN HAVE MEATH BEATEN KERRY IN THE CHAMPIONSHIP. NEVER HAVE THEY SEEN A KERRYMAN WITH A GREY FACE LIKE THIS. SEAN BOYLAN RAISES HIS HAND TO QUIETEN THE LAST OF HIS TEAM. PÁIDÍ BEGINS TO SPEAK: 'LAST TIME I WAS IN HERE IN A ROOM LIKE THIS, LADS, WAS IN 1998 WHEN THE BOLD MICKO BEAT US. THAT WAS A HARD ONE, LADS. TODAY IS SIMPLE, LADS. WE WERE BEATEN IN EVERY SECTOR OF THE FIELD — OUTCLASSED EVERYWHERE. YOU MADE THIS JOURNEY VERY EASY FOR ME TODAY, LADS. WHAT CAN WE SAY? WE WERE BEATEN.' GRACIOUS WORDS CAP AN EXTRAORDINARY DAY. KERRY, THE ALL IRELAND CHAMPIONS, BEATEN BY 15 POINTS. NOTHING MORE TO SAY.

ONE NEW STYLE JERSEY THERE'LL BE LITTLE DEMAND FOR. DONAL DALY OF KERRY, WEARING UNFAMILIAR WHITE AND GREEN, BLOCKS MEATH'S JOHN McDERMOTT DURING THE ALL IRELAND SEMI-FINAL.

HAVE YOU SEEN THAT SORT OF ENERGY BEFORE? SETANTA Ó HAILPÍN OF THE FAMOUS NORTHSIDE CORK AND FIJI HURLING FAMILY BURSTS THROUGH THE COMBINED DEFENCES OF GALWAY'S TONY ÓG REGAN AND CATHAL DERVAN IN THE ALL-IRELAND MINOR HURLING FINAL AT CROKE PARK.

STRANGEST STORY. IN THE MUNSTER HURLING FINAL UNDER A BLUE SKY, CORK WERE GIVEN A SHORT, SHARP HURLING LESSON BY TIPPERARY. BEATEN BY SIX POINTS IN A GAME WHERE ONLY ONE CORKMAN SCORED. AFTER THAT THEY JUST KEPT GETTING BETTER. HAMMERED WEXFORD. CAME BACK OFF THE ROPES AGAINST KILKENNY. AND BEAT GALWAY IN THE FINAL. HERE, TOMAS O'LEARY (SON OF THE GREAT CORNER-FORWARD SEÁNIE) LIFTS THE CUP. HIS COUNTERPART, GER FARRAGHER, HAD BEEN HOPING FOR HIS THIRD WINNER'S MEDAL IN SUCCESSION.

Guinness All-Ireland Hurling Final   **Tipperary 2-18 Galway 2-15**

CATHEDRAL.

IF GALWAY CAME TO CROKE PARK FOR THE ALL IRELAND FINAL IN SEPTEMBER
WITH A SHOCKINGLY YOUNG MIDFIELD, WELL, DAVID TIERNEY AND RICHIE
MURRAY HAD EARNED THEIR PASSAGE. THEY JUST HADN'T MET HUNGER LIKE
TIPPERARY'S. HERE, RICHIE MURRAY GETS ROBBED AS MAN OF THE MATCH
TOMMY DUNNE AND A SMILING DAVID KENNEDY GET ASH TO THE BALL.

September 9

September 9

Guinness All-Ireland Hurling Final   **Tipperary 2-18 Galway 2-15**

Tipperary 2-18 Galway 2-15   Guinness All-Ireland Hurling Final

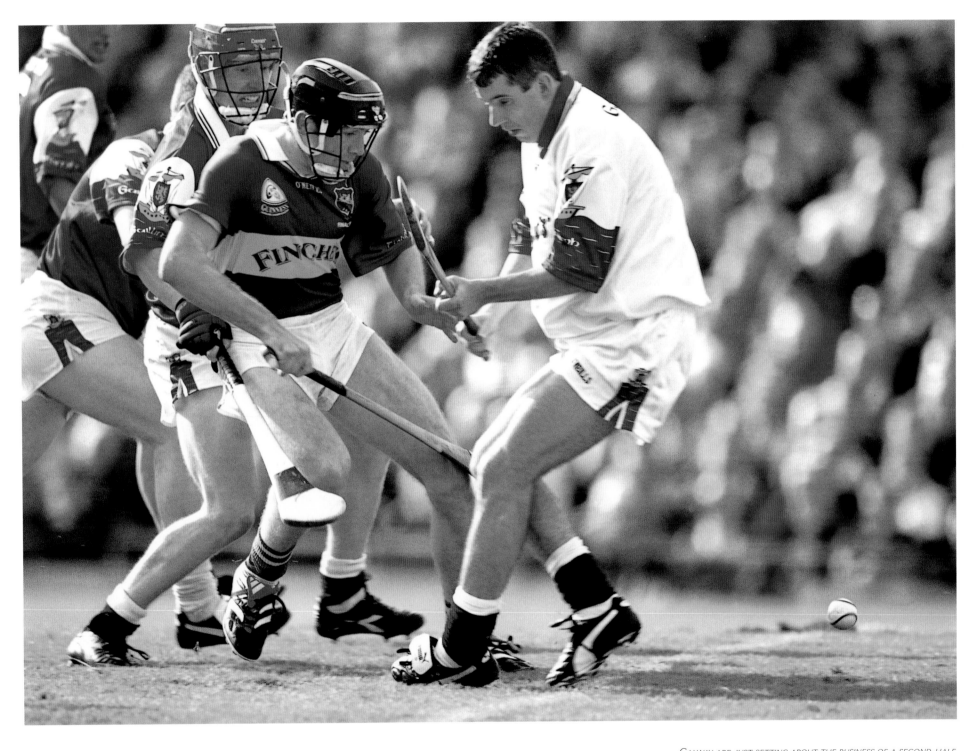

MARK O'LEARY PLAYED THE ALL IRELAND FINAL WITH A QUIET ASSURANCE THAT NEVER HINTED AT THE FLASHY FIGURES HE WOULD HAVE IN BRACKETS AFTER HIS NAME. SCORER OF 2-1, HE CELEBRATES HIS FIRST GOAL.

GALWAY ARE JUST SETTING ABOUT THE BUSINESS OF A SECOND-HALF COMEBACK WHEN MARK O'LEARY SOMEHOW SMUGGLES THE BALL PAST THEIR DEFENCE AND GOALKEEPER MICHAEL CRIMMINS.

Guinness All-Ireland Hurling Final   **Tipperary 2-18 Galway 2-15**

TOMMY DUNNE GREW UP IN A HURLING HOUSEHOLD, A HOME WHERE THE
BACK GARDEN WAS A FIELD FOR PLAYING IN AND DREAMING IN. THIS WAS
WHAT HE AND HIS BROTHERS DREAMED OF — TOMMY DUNNE BECOMING
THE FIRST TOOMEVARA MAN TO LIFT THE LIAM MACCARTHY CUP SINCE
MATT HASSETT 40 YEARS AGO. 'YOU GIVE YOUR LIFE TO PLAYING HURLING,'
TOMMY SAID ON ALL IRELAND FINAL DAY. 'I'VE BEEN HURLING FOR TIPP FOR
EIGHT YEARS AND HAVE NOTHING TO SHOW EXCEPT A COUPLE OF LEAGUE
MEDALS. THIS MAKES EVERYTHING WORTHWHILE.'

TIPPERARY'S GOLDEN SON. MANY DAYS NICKY ENGLISH HAS BEEN HOISTED ON THE SHOULDERS OF HIS COUNTYFOLK BUT NONE OF THEM WAS LIKE THIS. RELEASE. 'IN LIFE, IF YOU KEEP BANGING YOUR HEAD OFF A STONE WALL YOU'LL GET A BREAK,' SAYS NICKY.

September 9

SUDDENLY, IN EARLY SUMMER, POSSIBILITIES BLOSSOMED FOR ALAN KERINS. HE WAS ADDED TO THE COUNTY FOOTBALL PANEL AND BY AUGUST PEOPLE WERE SPEAKING OF HIM TAKING HOME ALL IRELAND MEDALS IN BOTH CODES. TIPPERARY INTERVENED BEFORE THE PRESSURE CAME. ALAN KERINS TAKES A RUNNERS-UP MEDAL HOME FROM THE ALL IRELAND HURLING FINAL.

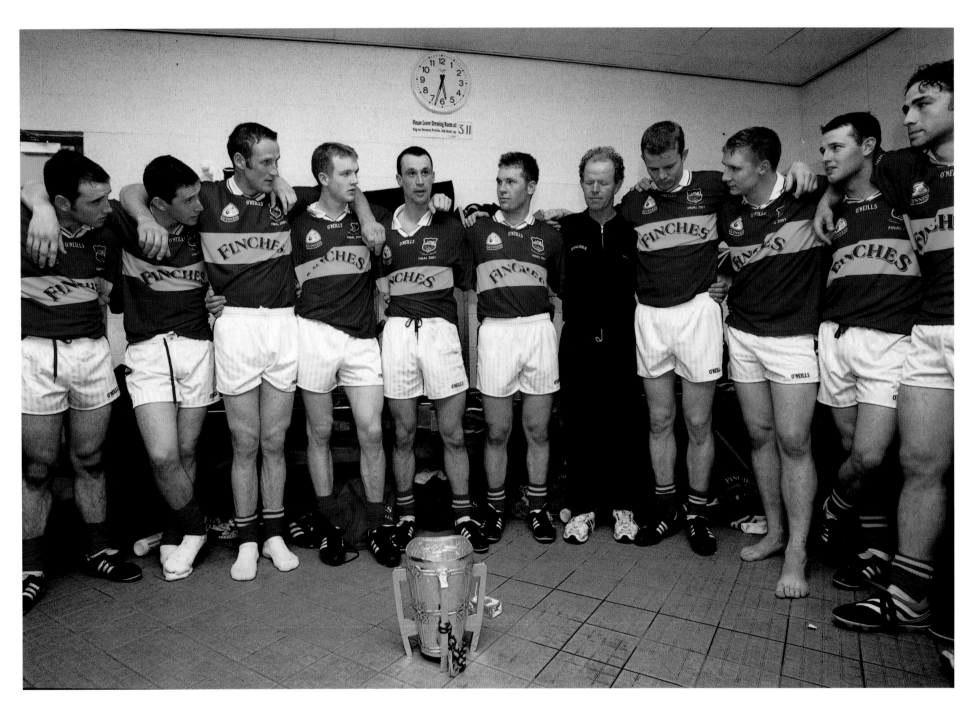

WHERE WE'VE BEEN AND WHERE WE ARE. TIPPERARY CAPTAIN TOMMY DUNNE SPEAKS TO HIS PLAYERS NOT LONG AFTER THE ALL IRELAND FINAL ENDS.

Foras na Gaeilge All-Ireland Junior Camogie Final   **Tipperary 4-16 Offaly 1-07**

*TIPPERARY ARE RIDING A WAVE AND THE OFFALY
JUNIOR CAMOGIE TEAM JUST GOT SWEPT AWAY.
CARINA CARROLL ABSORBS THE IMPACT.*

AND STILL THEY COME. MORE TIPPERARY JERSEYS IN CROKE PARK AS THE COUNTY SENIOR CAMOGIE TEAM TAKE THE FIELD FOR THE ALL IRELAND FINAL.

Foras na Gaeilge All-Ireland Senior Camogie Final   **Tipperary 4-13 Kilkenny 1-06**

STORY OF THE AFTERNOON. IN A PATTERN REPLICATED ALL ROUND THE FIELD, TIPPERARY'S CLAIRE MADDEN IS FIRST TO THE BALL. KILKENNY'S CATHERINE DOHERTY GIVES CHASE.

MORE SILVERWARE FOR THE SIDEBOARD IN THE SELF-PROCLAIMED HOME OF HURLING. TIPPERARY CAPTAIN EMILY HAYDEN LIFTS THE SENIOR CAMOGIE CUP.

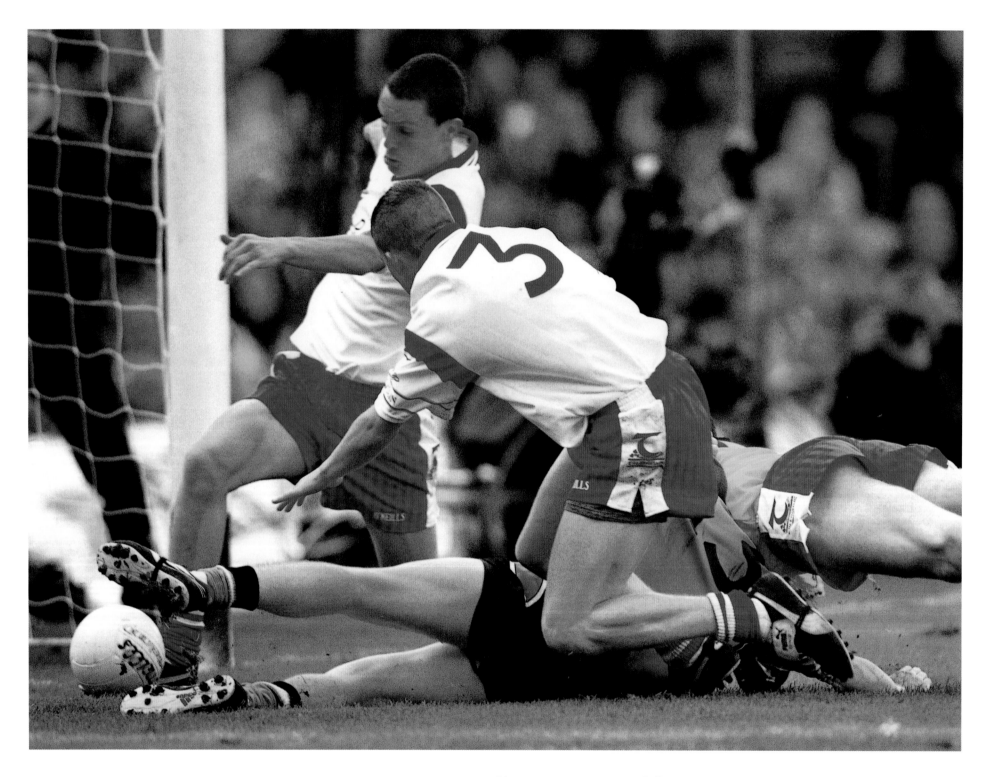

'How would you like your goal, Sir?'
'Late and with jam on it please.'
With almost the last act of the game, Dublin's David O'Callaghan somehow nudges the ball over the Tyrone goal-line to secure Dublin an unlikely draw in the All Ireland minor football final.

Tyrone 0-15 Dublin 1-12 All-Ireland Minor Football Final

*SO CLOSE TO TELLING HIS CHÁIRDE JUST HOW MUCH ÁTHAS
ACCEPTING AN CORN GAVE HIM. TYRONE MINOR CAPTAIN
PETER DONNELLY LEAVES HIS SPEECH FOR ANOTHER DAY
AFTER DUBLIN'S LATE GOAL IN CROKE PARK.*

Bank of Ireland All-Ireland Football Final **Galway 0-17 Meath 0-08**

Galway 0-17 Meath 0-08   Bank of Ireland All-Ireland Football Final

September 23

ANTICIPATION, SPECIFIC...

ANTICIPATION, GENERAL...

Bank of Ireland All-Ireland Football Final   **Galway 0-17 Meath 0-08**

PRESIDENT MARY MCALEESE SHAKES HANDS WITH MEATH'S OLLIE MURPHY.

THE PLAYER WILL LATER RETIRE FROM THE MATCH WITH A HAND INJURY.

Galway 0-17 Meath 0-08 Bank of Ireland All-Ireland Football Final

September 23

MOMENTS OF SHARED SILENCE IN CROKE PARK AS
THE DEAD AND INJURED OF THE SEPTEMBER 11
ATTACKS ON THE USA ARE REMEMBERED.

Bank of Ireland All-Ireland Football Final   **Galway 0-17 Meath 0-08**

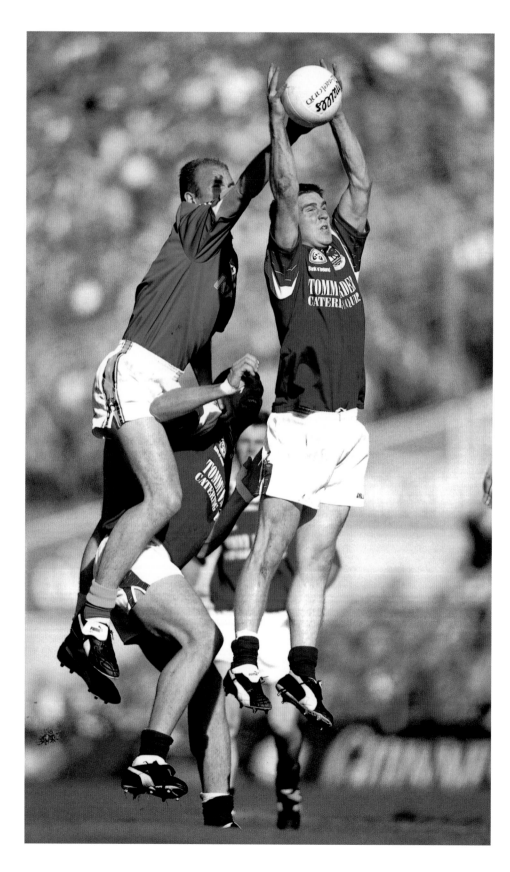

*JOHN MCDERMOTT OF MEATH
CLIMBS ABOVE GALWAY'S KEVIN
WALSH TO CONTEST A HIGH
BALL WITH PAUL CLANCY.*

JOE BERGIN OF GALWAY PACKED SEVERAL YEARS OF EXPERIENCE INTO THE SEASON JUST PAST. HE FINISHED AS AN ESTABLISHED FIRST TEAM PLAYER. HERE, HE CELEBRATES SCORING A POINT IN THE ALL IRELAND FINAL.

Bank of Ireland All-Ireland Football Final   **Galway 0–17 Meath 0-08**

*LAST OF THE SUMMER WINE. FRANK HUGHES
ON HIS FINAL DAY OF WORK AT CROKE PARK
AS A GAMES OFFICIAL.*

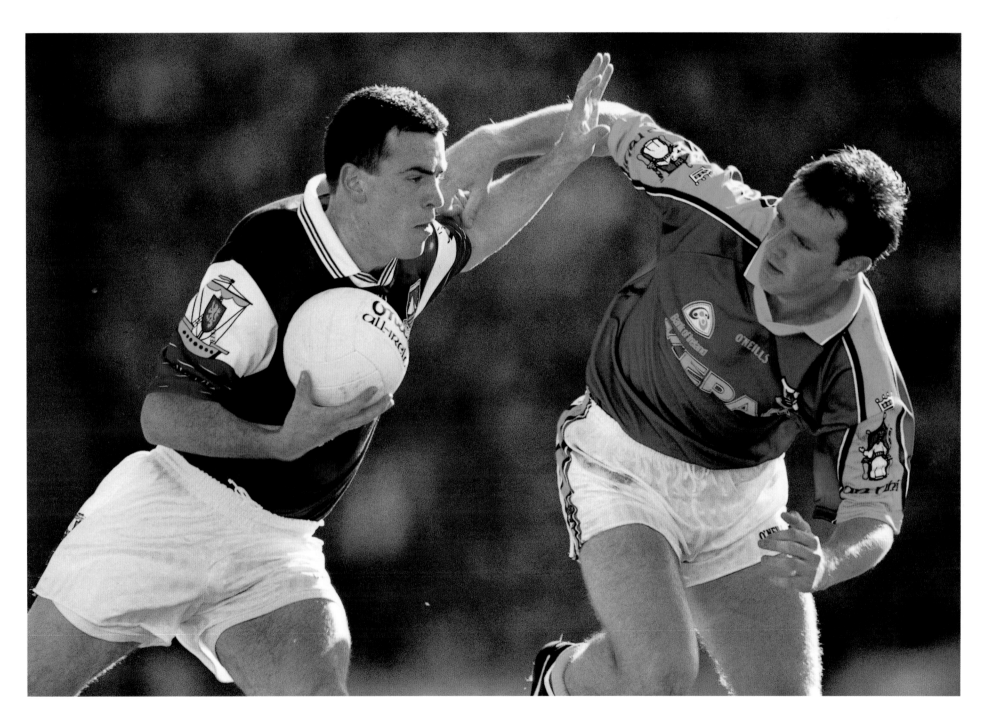

PADRAIG JOYCE'S ALL IRELAND FINAL HAD AN INAUSPICIOUS BEGINNING. THE FIRST FEW BALLS ADDRESSED TO HIM WERE INTERCEPTED BY DARREN FAY. FOR A WHILE JOYCE THOUGHT FAY'S BROAD SHOULDERS WERE ALL HE WOULD SEE IN CROKE PARK ON THIS DAY. 'I WAS LOOKING OVER TO THE SIDELINE SEEING IF THEY'D PUT UP THE NUMBER 14 TO TAKE ME OFF. NOTHING WENT RIGHT. LUCKILY HE LEFT ME ON.' LUCKILY. PADRAIG WORKED HIS WAY TO PROMINENCE. ONCE HE FOUND HIS RHYTHM HE SCORED TEN POINTS AND ESCHEWED A FINE GOAL CHANCE. 'WE SAY IN GALWAY IF IT'S NOT GOING WELL YOU CAN SURRENDER OR YOU CAN PUT YOUR SHOULDER TO THE WHEEL. THERE'S NO EXCUSE THOUGH FOR COMING OFF WITHOUT SWEATING.'

ONE OF THOSE DAYS. TREVOR GILES SENDS ALAN KEANE THE WRONG WAY BUT SLIPS HIS PENALTY THE WRONG SIDE OF THE POST.

Galway 0-17 Meath 0-08   Bank of Ireland All-Ireland Football Final

NOBODY'S ACHIEVEMENT THIS CHAMPIONSHIP SUMMER WAS GREATER THAN JOHN O'MAHONY'S. THE BALLAGHADEREEN MAN SOLDERED BACK TOGETHER A BROKEN TEAM EARLY IN THE CHAMPIONSHIP AND HIS HANDIWORK WAS TESTED MORE STRENUOUSLY EACH SUCCESSIVE DAY THEREAFTER. TRIUMPH MOVED HIM INTO THE VERY TOP RANK OF GAELIC FOOTBALL MANAGERS. HERE, HE CELEBRATES WITH PADRAIG JOYCE.

Bank of Ireland All-Ireland Football Final   **Galway 0-17 Meath 0-08**

PLEASANT DUTIES.
GARY FAHEY LIFTS THE SAM
MAGUIRE FOR GALWAY.

PETER DONNELLY HAS HIS MOMENT AT LAST. HE LIFTS THE IRISH PRESS CUP ON BEHALF OF THE TYRONE MINOR FOOTBALL TEAM AFTER THEY DEFEATED DUBLIN IN THE REPLAYED FINAL AT BREFFNI PARK, CAVAN.

TG4 All-Ireland Ladies Junior Football Final   **Roscommon 1-18 Kildare 0-08**

*THE PATTERN OF WESTERN FOOTBALL
DOMINANCE LOOKS SET TO CONTINUE AS
ROSCOMMON'S EIMEAR CASEY SCORES
HER SIDE'S ONLY GOAL IN THEIR 11-POINT
WIN OVER KILDARE AT CROKE PARK.*

*ROSCOMMON CAPTAIN MARY BEADES
LIFTS THE ALL IRELAND JUNIOR TROPHY.*

TG4 All-Ireland Ladies Senior Football Final   **Laois 2-14 Mayo 1-16**

A FANCY FOR MAYO. EIGHT-YEAR-OLD LEWIS AFULOGUN OF SCOIL CARMEL, FIRHOUSE, CO. DUBLIN, AWAITS THE ARRIVAL OF THE MAYO TEAM ONTO THE PITCH AT CROKE PARK.

BIG GAME BALLET. JACKIE MORAN OF MAYO AND GRAINNE DUNNE OF LAOIS ARE FROZEN IN MOTION AS THEY CONTEST AN EARLY BALL IN CROKE PARK.

TG4 All-Ireland Ladies Senior Football Final   **Laois 2-14 Mayo 1-16**

CLIFFHANGER. SECONDS BEFORE THE HOOTER GOES IN CROKE PARK AND THE TEAMS ARE DEADLOCKED. THEN THE MAYO DEFENCE MAKES A FATAL ERROR. GOALIE DENISE HORAN TAKES A SHORT KICK-OUT TO STAR FORWARD CORA STAUNTON. CORA, HOWEVER, IS INSIDE THE 20-METRE LINE. REFEREE MARTIN DUFFY BLOWS FOR A FREE. IT FALLS TO MARY KIRWAN TO TAKE THE LAST KICK OF THE GAME. HER CONCENTRATION NEVER WAVERS…

…UNTIL THE HOOTER SOUNDS.

TG4 All-Ireland Ladies Senior Football Final   **Laois 2-14   Mayo 1-16**

Laois 2-14 Mayo 1-16 TG4 All-Ireland Ladies Senior Football Final

MAYO'S STAR FORWARD CORA STAUNTON CLINGS TO THE CROKE PARK GRASS AS HER TEAM'S BID FOR THREE ALL IRELANDS IN A ROW ENDS.

LAOIS HAVE THEIR OWN STORY. THEY HAVE PLAYED IN SEVEN ALL IRELAND FINALS PRIOR TO THIS AND LOST THEM ALL. ONE WOMAN, SUE RAMSBOTTOM, PLAYED ON SIX OF THOSE LOSING TEAMS. SO WHEN LAOIS CAPTAIN ANGELA CASEY LIFTS THE CUP, SHE DOES SO ON BEHALF OF ALL THOSE WHO CONTRIBUTED TO THIS MOMENT.

Foster's International Rules Series   **Australia 1-13-08 Ireland 2-13-08**

Australia 1-13-07 Ireland 2-17-08   Foster's International Rules Series

HAPPY RETURNS. ANTHONY TOHILL OF DERRY, ONCE A TRAINEE PLAYER WITH THE MELBOURNE DEMONS, RETURNS YEARS LATER AS CAPTAIN OF IRELAND TO SCORE HIS NATION'S FIRST GOAL IN THE FIRST INTERNATIONAL RULES SERIES TEST AT THE MCG.

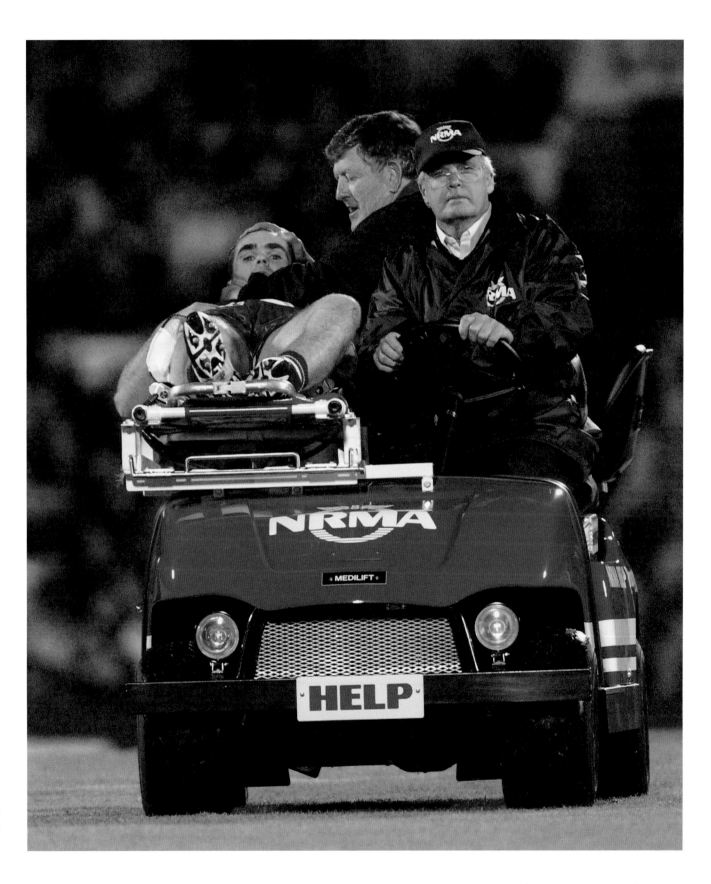

THE HEROES, BORNE FROM THE BATTLEFIELD ON, EM, LITTLE BLUE GOLF CARTS. SEAN MARTIN LOCKHART IS REMOVED FROM THE ACTION IN ADELAIDE WHILE TEAM MEDIC DR FELIX MCKNIGHT TENDS TO HIM.

Foster's International Rules Series   **Australia 1-13-07 Ireland 2-17-08**

ALL OVER BAR THE SHOUTING. THE SECOND TEST WON BY A RECORD MARGIN, THE SERIES SAFE — ANTHONY TOHILL, THE IRISH PLAYERS AND THE MANAGEMENT TEAM GET THEIR HANDS ON THE SILVER AND PREPARE FOR AN EVENING WHEN ADELAIDE WILL BE PAINTED RED.

ONE THAT GOT AWAY. TADHG KENNELLY OF LISTOWEL EMMETS AND SYDNEY SWANS PROVED TO BE ONE OF THE PLAYERS OF THE SERIES, LEAVING GAELIC FOOTBALL TO LAMENT HIS MOVE DOWN UNDER. HERE, HE KEEPS ONE STEP AHEAD OF AUSTRALIA'S CHRIS SCOTT.

October 21

International Challenge   **New South Wales 1-14 Ireland 5-12**

AND THE SIREN SONG OF THE GAMES ALWAYS DRAWS YOU BACK. ON A HOT DAY IN SYDNEY, BRIAN MCENIFF ENTERS THE FRAY AND SCORES THE FINAL POINT OF AN EXHIBITION GAME. FOR THE RECORD, IT WAS A THING OF BEAUTY, 20 METRES OUT AND HUGGING THE SIDELINE. NO FINER WAY TO SAY GOODBYE. AND THANKS.